This book is to be returned on or before
the last date stamped below.

St Clements
Class 2

LOOK AROUND
THE SCHOOL

Clive Pace and Jean Birch

Illustrated by Steve Wheele

How to use this book

Use this book to help you discover things about your school. Try to find out as much as you can. The answers to some of the questions are at the back of the book, but don't look at them until you have tried to work them out for yourself. Some of the questions only you can answer because they are about your school.

Never leave your classroom or school without first telling an adult where you are going. Never talk to strangers.

Look Around You

Look Around Homes
Look Around the Park
Look Around the School
Look Around Shops
Look Around the Street
Look Around Transport

Editor: Marcella Streets
Designer: Ross George

First published in 1988 by
Wayland (Publishers) Ltd
61 Western Road, Hove
East Sussex, BN3 1JD, England

© Copyright 1988 Wayland (Publishers) Ltd

British Library Cataloguing in Publication Data
Pace, Clive
    The school.
    1. Schools — For children
    I. Title   II. Birch, Jean   III. Series
    371

    ISBN 1 85210 469 4

Phototypeset by Kalligraphics Ltd, Horley, Surrey
Printed and bound in Belgium by Casterman S.A.

Contents

Answers to questions are on page 28.
All the words that are <u>underlined</u> appear
in the glossary on page 29.

THE SCHOOL NAME

What is your school's name?

Schools are often called after a person, the street they stand in, or the <u>district</u> they are in.

How did your school get its name?

The name will be on a sign somewhere around the building.

Do you know where the sign is?

Look carefully at the sign.

What other <u>information</u> is on it?

Does the sign tell you who owns your school?

Most schools are owned by <u>Local Education Authorities</u>. Their badge, or logo, might be on your school sign.

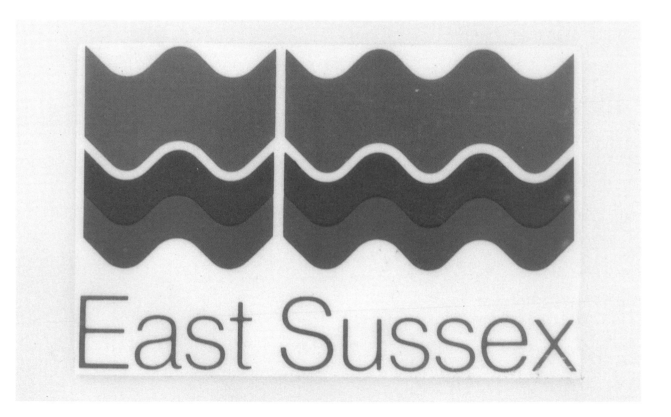

Make a list of other buildings in your town where you can see the logo.

THE SCHOOL BUILDING

Look carefully at the outside of your school.
Does it look like either of these?

This school was built almost 100 years ago.

Notice how big and high it is.

This school was built only a few years ago. It is a very modern style.

There are many different styles of school, depending on when and where the schools were built.

Try to find out how old your school is.
Are there any different kinds of school nearby?
Can you guess when they were built?

BUILDING MATERIALS

When people built schools, they often used materials that were popular at the time. So sometimes you can guess the age of a school from the sort of <u>building material</u> it is made of.

Do you know what the materials below are?

 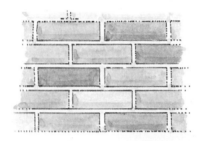 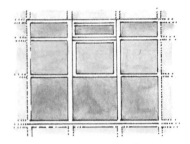

Twenty years ago, builders ▶ used a lot of concrete.

Today brick is more popular.

What is your school built of?

Are the same materials used for other buildings nearby?

Another common material found in schools is glass.

School windows come in many different shapes and sizes. Most modern schools have rectangular windows. They are cheap and easy to make.

The door in this photograph has glass in it.
Do you know why the glass has wire in it?

Draw pictures of the different shapes of windows you can see in your school.

THE SCHOOL ENTRANCE

Look outside your school gate or main <u>entrance</u>.

Is there a <u>barrier</u> on the pavement like this?

Can you guess what it is for?

How many entrances are there to your school?

Many years ago, girls and boys used to have separate entrances. You can still see the signs at some schools.

Today boys and girls usually use the same entrance.

Is there an entrance to your school that you are not allowed to use?

If so, who uses it?

◀ This back entrance is being used to deliver school dinners.

THE SCHOOL PLAN

If you could see your school from up above, what shape do you think it would be?

Some schools have a <u>regular</u> shape like the one below.
▼

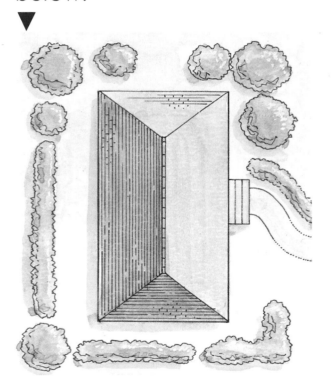

Other schools are more <u>irregular</u> in shape like this one.
▼

You can find out the shape of your school by looking at a plan of it. Your head teacher might have one you could look at. If not, you could draw one.

Some modern schools are open plan. This means that there are very few walls between the different areas of the school. Sometimes there are no walls between the classrooms.

Can you think of any <u>disadvantages</u> of an open-plan school?
Are there any <u>advantages</u>?

THE SCHOOL PLAYGROUND

Most schools have a playground made of grass, <u>tarmac</u> or concrete.

This school has both tarmac and grass.
What is your playground made of?

▶

Playgrounds often have special markings on them.
Do you know what these markings are for?

Make a list of all the games you play in your playground.

Ask your teachers what their favourite playground games were when they were your age. You may find they liked the same games.

Is there any play equipment in your playground?
Some play equipment can be dangerous.
Do you know why?

THE BOILER ROOM

How is your school kept warm?

You may have noticed radiators or heaters in your classroom, but do you know how they are kept warm?

▶

Ask your teacher if you can look around the school boiler room. This caretaker is checking a boiler.

▼

What else is in your school boiler room?

◄ This is a timer.

Do you know what it is for?

Do you know what this is?

You may have seen one at home too.

FIRE SAFETY IN SCHOOL

Fire and smoke can kill very quickly. It is important to know exactly what to do if a fire starts.

Would you know what to do if a fire started in your school?

Find out from your teacher.

How many fire alarms are there in your school?

Do they look like these?

Find out which alarm is nearest to your classroom. Ask your teacher how to work it.

Do you know what this is? What is it for? ▶

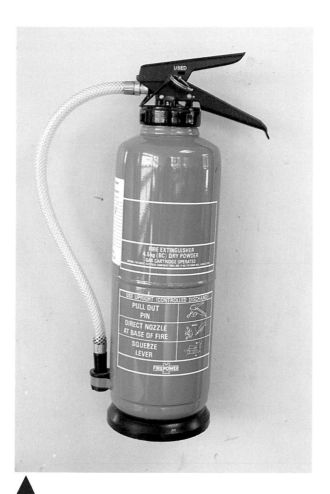

▲

Have you noticed the <u>fire extinguishers</u> in your school? What colour are they? Are they all the same colour?

Never play with fire alarms or extinguishers. They can save lives.

GETTING RID OF RUBBISH

Where are your school's dustbins?

They are usually within easy reach of the kitchen, so that left-over food can be thrown away easily.

Schools use different kinds of dustbin. This bin is used for food only. ►

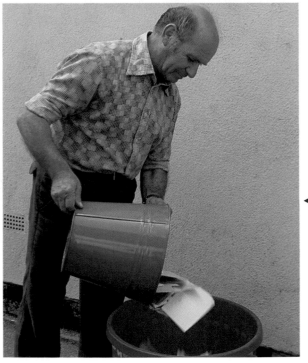

◄ A different bin is used for other rubbish. The caretakers and cleaners empty the classroom wastepaper bins into a big dustbin after school.

Some rubbish can be burned in the school grounds.

▲
This caretaker is burning
rubbish in an <u>incinerator</u>.

This school has a large
amount of rubbish. The
rubbish is put in a <u>skip.</u>
When the skip is full, it will
be taken away by a lorry.

▶

NOTICES AND SIGNS

There are all sorts of notices and signs around a school. They give information or tell you what to do.

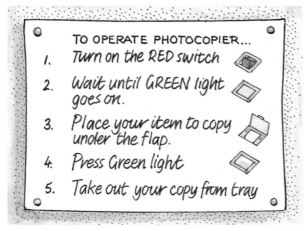

TO OPERATE PHOTOCOPIER...
1. Turn on the RED switch
2. Wait until GREEN light goes on.
3. Place your item to copy under the flap.
4. Press Green light
5. Take out your copy from tray

▲

This notice gives <u>instructions</u>.

HEAD MISTRESS
Ms A Singh

▲

This notice gives information. You can tell whose room this is by reading the sign.

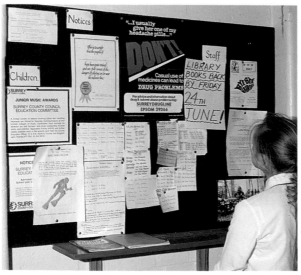

◀ Some of the information on this board is for parents.

The screen on this computer tells the children how to use it.

What sort of notices and signs are there in your school?

What did you find out?

Page 12:
Pebble-dashing
Brick
Panel and glass

Page 13:
The glass in the door has **wire** in it so that it does not shatter easily in the heat of a fire, or if someone falls against it.

Page 14:
The **barrier** helps to stop children from running out of school on to the road.

Page 18:
The **markings** are for hopscotch.

Page 19:
If you fall off play equipment on to a hard surface you can hurt yourself.

Page 20:
The school boiler pumps hot water to the **radiators** through pipes.

Page 21:
The caretaker sets the **timer** so that the heating comes on and goes off at the right times.
This is an **electricity meter**. It measures how much electricity is used.

Page 23:
This is a **fire blanket**. It can be put over a fire, for example a chip pan fire in the school kitchen. It puts out the flames by stopping the oxygen in the air from getting to them.

There might be red, green, blue and black **fire extinguishers** in your school. The red ones contain water. They are used to put out paper or wood fires. Black fire extinguishers are for electrical fires. They make a very loud noise when you use them. Green and blue extinguishers are for all sorts of fires. The contents of the black and green extinguishers are very cold and can hurt your skin.

Glossary

Advantages   The good points about
   something.
Barrier   Metal railings that stop people
   going out into the road.
Building material   Something used to
   make a building.
Disadvantages   The bad points about
   something.
District   Part of a county or town.
Entrance   The way in.
Fire extinguishers   Large metal containers.
   When you squirt the contents at a fire,
   they can put it out.
Incinerator   A container in which things
   are burned to ashes.
Information   Facts.
Instruction   Words that tell you what to do.
Irregular   Not even.
Local Education Authority   The people
   whose job it is to look after the schools in
   a town or area.
Regular   An even shape, like a square.
Skip   A large container for rubbish.
Tarmac   A mixture of crushed stones, tar
   and bitumen.

Further reading

The Class Teacher by Diana Bentley
(Wayland, 1987)
The Dinner Ladies by Diana Bentley
(Wayland, 1987)
The School Caretaker by Diana Bentley
(Wayland, 1987)
The School Secretary by Diana Bentley
(Wayland, 1987)
The Teacher by Anne Stewart (Ladybird,
1986)

For older readers:

Exploring Buildings by Ralph Whitlock
(Wayland, 1987)
Exploring Schools by Sallie Purkis
(Wayland, 1988)
School Days by Penny Marshall
(Macdonald, 1984)

Picture Acknowledgements

Cephas 8, 10, 13, 14, 20 (top), 21 (top), 22 (right and left) 24 (left), 26, 27; Sally and
Richard Greenhill 17, 18 (top), 19; C. L. Pace 11, 12, 25 (bottom); Sefton 21 (bottom);
Wayland Picture Library 9, 15 (bottom), 18 (bottom), 20 (bottom), 24 (right), 25 (top); Zefa
15 (top).

Index